# Learn the Fu
## & Basics of Fun
## Different Sports to Play

*By Vince Stead*

# LEARN THE FUNDAMENTALS & BASICS OF FUN DIFFERENT SPORTS TO PLAY

ISBN:  978-1468070460

www.VinceStead.com

# 1. Golf: The Elements of Playing Golf

The origin of golf in Scotland and was enjoyed from 15<sup>th</sup> century. The game was encouraged by the king of England James VI in 1603. In 1721, Golf was regularly played on Glasgow green, and the first Golf club and rules were laid in 1744. The first rules were written by Edinburgh golfers, and the first golf club was the honorable company of Edinburgh golfers. Saint Andrew is the name of the very first golf course situated in Scotland.

Understanding the game: The game is played by the competing players also termed as golfers with different types of clubs and balls. The club is a long stick with a grip on one head and a club on the bottom end. The player makes a grip on the upper head and hit is the ball with the help of the club to put them in the series of holes that are created on a golf course. Clubs are made from different materials like wood and expensive metals sometimes.

Golf courses: A golf course is consisting of a number of holes. These holes are arranged like a series, and each of the series comprises of teeing ground, rough, fairway and other hazards that a golfer has to cross with full power and courage.

Some of the area of the golf course is green with a flag-stick sticking up and a cup at the bottom of the flag. Most golf courses have 18 holes because a standard round of golf is actually based on 18 holes. The numbers of holes can be increased and decrease in many other courses. Some of them have nine holes and some of them have 27 or 36 holes.

Teeing ground or tee is the area from where the game is started or from where the first shot is placed. The area between the tee and putting green is called the fairway where the grass is very short and is considering the most advantageous area. Rough is the area, which is considered as disadvantageous and creates a problem for the golfer in hitting the ball.

Par: Par represents the number of strokes that a good golfer should try to hit the ball in that many times or less. In professional golf tournaments, par is considered the central component of the game. Par three, four and five holes are very common in most courses; however, there are some courses with par six holes. The distance for men and women varies. Par three men are equal to 250 yards and par three women are 210 yards.

Basic rules of golf:  Many people love to play golf but most of them are found unaware of the rules.  Rules are adding more charm and fun to the game of golf. Other basic rules are to avoiding disturbing the golfer by chatting and standing close to him/her.  Play in a quick manner and try to minimize the number of strokes.  Never put your club in the putting green.  Before starting, you must read the international and standardized rules as well as local rules. Count your clubs before starting the actual game and make sure that the number of clubs must be fourteen in all.

# 2. Hockey: A Very Interesting Sport

Hockey is a very interesting and popular game. There are many types of hockey. However, the most popular one is field hockey. Field hockey is the national sport of Pakistan and India. Other types of hockey sports are ice hockey, floor hockey, sledge hockey, Inline hockey, roller hockey and street hockey. This sport is played by two teams and in each team, there are eleven players.

History: It is not clear where the origin of the hockey is from, however, in the histories of many countries a game or sport with curved sticks was found. In the histories of Egypt, ancient Greece, Mongolia, China and Ireland, the evidence of hockey like a sport has been found. This has shown that hockey is an ancient sport.

Understanding of the game: There is a very slight difference in the rules of field hockey and other types of hockey. Field hockey is the game, which is played on the natural land and grass. The game is based on two 35-minutes halves. Each of both teams is having intentions to make the goal against each other. There are two-goal lines placed at the ends of both ends of the field.

The team members of each team use the sticks to push the ball and when they reach to the semicircle of opposite team's goal area, they hit the ball in to make a goal. They must use the curved head to push the ball otherwise; it will count as a foul. Every member of the team should respect the umpires as well as avoid hitting any of the members of the opposite team. Never hit the ball in a manner that will make it rise above your knees or 18 inches.

Common fouls: Every sport has its own rules. In hockey, the breaches of these rules are called fouls. Mostly fouls are caused because of the misunderstanding of referees or umpires signals and unawareness of the rules. Ask about the signal if you cannot be able to understand but ask politely because in case of misbehaving; they will call you for penalties.

Penalty calls are actually a kind of punishment during the game that results in the breakage of any kind of rule. Penalty corner is a type of foul that is made inside the shooting circle. Another common foul is making foot contact to the ball, and it is termed as a penalty for a foot call. Each time a player gets a foul, it will result in the advantage of the opposite team. So try to play carefully.

Suggestions for a successful game: For a successful game, every player of the hockey team must understand the rules and regulations of the game. The player should build up self-efficacy and passion and always try to respect the referee. Make a distance between the stick and foot as it will help you in the reduction of foot fouls.

Make a correct grip on the hockey stick in a manner that the right hand should be placed in a relaxed style than that of the left. The distance between the hands should be 5 ½ inches to 7 inches. There are many guidebooks available in the market as well as on the internet that are written by famous and experienced players. You can get guidance and help by reading some of their strategy stories.

# 3. Tennis: A Good Way to Stay Active and Fit

Tennis is a very famous game in which there are usually two players or between four players in the shape of teams, two members on each team. If you look at the history, you will find that the history of this game is based on several thousand years.

Some believe that the game has come from ancient Egyptians, Romans and Greeks. However, another believe is that it is actually introduced by European monks. They used to play tennis in their religious gathering and ceremonies for entertainment. However, it is not complete and accurate as there are some other believes also present in the world. Modern tennis was actually born in 1874, in London, England.

The equipment has and courts: If you want to play a game you will need certain equipment, without which you cannot play, they are a racquet and a rubber ball. The racquet is a metallic frame with a wide hoop in which networks of fine strings are stretched. This frame is also available in wood. In the beginning, tennis courts were very different as compared to today's modern courts. In the early days, lawn courts were popular for this game however, with the passage of time indoor courts took the place and popularity of open-air courts.

Rules and regulations of the game: If you are playing with your friend just to pass the time, then you need no kinds of rules and can play it in a way, which you like best. However, if you love this game and want to play it like professionals, then there are certain rules, which you have to follow. The rules are as follows:

The player must have a racquet of a good quality with unbroken and tight strings.

The player should show respect and courtesy for all the judges in both the situations that are success or failure. The breach of this rule leads to a punishment from fine to suspension of the player. The severity of punishment is directly proportional to the severity of the breach.

The player must properly dress with empty pickets.

In the tennis court, there are some boundary lines; the player should make all the services from behind the boundary lines.

The submission of drug test before starting the game is necessary.

Tennis shoes are also important to put on as they help in the protection of a tennis court from blemishes and other type of damage.

Tennis is a continuous play sport with duration of 2 hours; however, it goes for 3 hours in cases of woman's play and 5 hours in case of men's play. There are different methods for keeping score of the game. At the startup of the game, when both the players have zero scores, it is called as love all. The first point is referred to as "15" the second score is "30" the third is "40" and the fourth one is called "Game". When the score of both players reach to three points then it is termed as 'Deuce'.

# 4. Tennis: Another Example of the Game

Tennis is a game where a player's skills have to be developed with the proper practice. Playing tennis can be a tiring and demanding task, but knowing the sport entirely, including the method of playing and scoring system can make it an enjoyable game. One of the more important aspects of tennis is learning how to serve properly. It can help you win many points; it is meant to give you an advantage. Serving should be forceful, fast and should be done in a way that your opponent will not be able to return it.

In serving the tennis ball, you have to be positioned behind the baseline, in a sideways stance. You use your right hand to toss up the ball, while your left hand holds the racket. You should throw the ball straight upward, ideally at the height of 18". It is not right to toss the ball overhead, rather from a distance that is 1-foot ahead of your right leg, the part of your body that is nearest to the baseline. Serve the ball diagonally opposite, to the court of the opponent. It is recommended to serve the ball from the highest point that you can reach, to help increase the success rate of your serve. Serving is the first step that you should master in playing tennis.

When you serve the tennis ball, it is covered by restriction to fall in a specific place. The return shot is different. You can return the shot in any place in your opponent's court. However, it should not fall on the stripes that are on the courtsides. In tennis, there are two types of strokes:

Ground strokes – are strokes played from the baseline

Valley shots – are strokes where you have to approach the net.

When you play a shot over the head of your opponent who approaches the net, this is called lob shot. It will cause your rival to run back so he takes control of his shot. Playing lob shots will allow you to gain advantage over your rival player. However, you should play this shot properly; otherwise, your opponent will have the chance to smash the tennis ball. It will be a great help if you have knowledge of the measurements of the court, as well as the different tennis terms.

Examples of some tennis terms are forehand and backhand. These terms are classifications of how you hold the racket. Forehand is a term used when you hold the racket with your palm facing the ball? Backhand is the term when you do it the other way around.

Once you have an understanding of the basic rules in playing tennis, you can play it better.

# 5. Soccer: How to Play Soccer

Soccer is a game that is played according to a set of rules termed as Laws of the Game. A single ball (soccer ball) is used in playing soccer, and participated in by two teams. Each team consists of 11 players; these two teams compete in getting the soccer ball into the opponent's goal. This makes the goal score. The team that succeeds scoring more goals is declared the winner at the end of the game.

If the two teams, however, scored an equal number of goals, the game will be declared a tie. This may not be applicable during championship games where there should be a declared winner. An example of this situation is the World Cup Finals. It will not certainly end in a tie. There will be overtime in this case.

The first rule in playing soccer is that players should not touch the ball with their arms or hands during play. The goalkeepers are exempted from this rule, and hands are used in throwing the ball during a restart. Players should use their feet to move the ball around, and they may also use the other parts of their bodies, except the hands/arms. In a typical soccer game, the ball is propelled towards the other team's goal through various actions, such as passing the ball to a team member, dribbling, or taking a shot at the goal. This is strictly guarded by the rival team's goalkeeper. Except for the goalkeeper, there are three main categories in the soccer player positions, namely Strikers or Forwards, who are tasked of scoring goals. Defenders, who should prevent their opponent team from scoring.

Midfielders, who dispose of the opponents and keep possession of the soccer ball for passing through to the forwards, these players are collectively called outfield players. There are 10 of them in a game, plus the single goalkeeper.  Players may also be differentiated by which side of the field he mostly stays. There can be central defenders, and right and left midfielders.

The 10 outfield players can be positioned in any combination, like four defenders, four midfielders and two forwards. It is also possible to have three defenders, three midfielders and four forwards. The number of players in each of these positions will determine the team's style of playing. However, players can switch position at any time during a play.

The layout or positioning of the soccer players on the pitch is usually called the team formation. The soccer team manager has the ability to change the team formation and all tactics and any time.

# 6. Basketball: A Team Sport

Basketball is played in a team, you can practice individually once in a while, but it is not a sport, which can be played individually. It consists of five players, each on both teams who try to throw or shoot the ball into the net of the opposite team, of course abiding by the rules of the game. American basketball is one of the most viewed and popular sports in the world.

The rim of the basketball hoop is 18 inches in diameter and it should be 10 feet above ground level fitted onto a backboard. 'Dribbling' is a common term used in the game of 'American basketball', if a player is good at dribbling, he is considered to be a useful player. Walking with the ball and hitting the ball with the leg unlike football is considered violation of the rules of the game. Height is of advantage in the game of 'American basketball'. In the game of basketball, the team that puts the maximum number of baskets into the opposition's hoop is considered the winner.

There are center, defense and offense players in the game of basketball too. The tallest ones are made center players, provided they are good at the game. The game starts off with a free throw and then it depends on the players of the respective teams to dribble the ball and pass it from one player to the other, because in this way you can reach the opposite team's goal post.

The basket of the opposite team is known as the goal post. Dribbling was not part of the original game of basketball, but later as the game evolved, dribbling was introduced; only passing the ball was considered part of the game. Association football was used initially to play basketball. The initial balls were brown in color too, but later in the 1950s, Tom Hinkle felt the need for a more visible ball in the game of 'American basketball' and hence introduced the orange ball, which is still prevalent until today.

Peach baskets were used as basketballs in yesteryear's, but now it has been replaced by backboards and metal hoops. If you learn the terms and rules associated with a sport and join a team, you should be able to do well in the sport, irrespective of the sport you want to play. Similarly, 'American Basketball' requires determination and knowledge of the rules and regulations, a good coach and a good team and if you have all this nobody can stop you from becoming a renowned 'American Basketball player'.

# 7. Basketball: Another Example of the Game

There is an advantage in the game of basketball if you are tall because in this game, it involves the players bouncing the ball with the hands and tossing it into the basketball hoop high up above. When you are tall, it is much easier to throw the ball successfully into the hoop since you can jump higher. Of course, it is understood that there is no way of scoring points in basketball if you do not have an accurate shoot.

In order to fully understand the game, you need to at least watch a game first. You can find many basketball matches through sports channels and also through the Internet and you can learn a lot by watching the matches. Basically, basketball is an indoor sport game that is played with two teams playing opposite each other. Each team consists of about eleven or twelve basketball players with five players being on the court and their aim are to score as many points as possible within the period. A game of basketball match has four quarters with each quarter being about ten to twelve minutes long, depending which types of basketballs are played.

Normally, a basketball court has two basketball hoops of eighteen inches wide in diameter at opposite side, each rimmed hoop being mounted ten feet high on a backboard. A basketball player can only use his or her hands to play and he or she can pass the ball or bounce it while walking or running which is called 'dribbling'. It is considered against the rules to carry the ball while walking or running and this act is called 'traveling'. It is also considered foul play to double dribbling in which the player holds the ball only to resume dribbling.

In order to score points in basketball, the players have to shoot the ball into the ring. Two points are being awarded to the shooting team if the players are touching the hoop or inside the three-point line when shooting the ball. If the players throw the ball outside the three-point line and the ball falls inside the hoop, three points are rewarded to the shooting team. This kind of scoring is known as three-pointers. Should there be a tie, additional time might be awarded and the team with the most scores wins the match.

Players are always on their best behavior, as free throws will be given to the opponent team if the players are being fouled for bad sportsmanship or they were being fouled while shooting. For these fouls, a referee will be on the court to ensure a fair game.

# 8. Football: The Biggest Sport

American football is a big sport, but not that big that you cannot master the skill to play it, if you make up your mind to do so. It is a game played by 11 players on both teams. You make a goal, when you put the ball into the opposite team's goal post and if your team is successful in doing this, more number of times than the opposition team, then you and your team win the game.

First of all, you should understand the different aspects of the game, one of which is the field; the football field is 120 yards long, in which the playing field is of 100 yards. There are stripes made at 5 yards levels and shorter lines called hash lines and goal posts at the end of the field on both sides.

In the teams, there are players who play in offense, and then there are teams who play in defense and sometimes special teams. There are different players in the defense who are known as quarterback players, halfback players and fullback players in the offense category. In the defense category, there are players who belong to the linebacker category and the cornerback category. In the special team, there is a gunner, holder, kick returner, long snapper, placekicker, punter and a punt returner, in case there is a special team.

Before the game begins, you should know that the captains of both teams and the referee meet in the center of the field for the coin toss. The winner of the coin toss starts the game, either by receiving the ball from the opposite team by way of a kick-off or by kicking the ball to the opposite team.

There are four downs in a game of American football, right from the time the ball comes into play for the first time until the time the officials whistle is called one down and likewise there are four downs in the game of football.

Therefore, before playing 'American Football', it is better to know the terms, rules and regulations of the game etc. If you understand all this well and start taking proper coaching from a good coach then it should not be that difficult to play football, and of course, there should be a team to play with and play against, which is understood.

# 9. Football: Another Example of the Game

Football is one of the most popular sports in the world and everyone enjoys watching the game. When it comes to football, there is no discrimination to it and everyone, be it Asians or Caucasians, has a great time watching the match. There are many teams in the world and each country has its own leagues and many football clubs. For example, in England alone, there are a huge numbers of football associations and to name it all would be the sign of a great football fan.

Some of the famous football clubs in England are Manchester United, Arsenal, Chelsea, and Liverpool and so on. Then, once every four years, there is a World Cup where the top football teams would be fighting for the glory of being crowned the best football team.

There are many children who would grow up wanting to be a footballer, no thanks to the great exposure to the sport. Basically, in order to understand this game, all you have to do is just watch a match or two and have a football fan explain the game to you. It would be much easier to understand it this way. However, should you do not have a football fan friend, then all you need to do is just to read up on the rules and regulations of the game and watch a match or two. Pretty soon, you will be able to understand the game.

Normally, football is played on a rectangular field and there should be two teams of eleven football players on each team playing on the ground. The main idea of the game is to kick a round, spherical ball with their legs heading towards the opponents side and score a goal. In order to score a goal, the players have to kick the ball towards the goal post, which is guarded by the opponent's goalkeeper whose main job is to stop the other team from scoring a goal. At the end of the game, the team with the most goals wins.

Besides the eleven players from each team on the field, there are also a few referees that will be monitoring the game constantly. Their purpose on the field is to ensure that there is no foul play and both teams play honestly. They also determine whether the players make any mistakes or if the moves made by the players to possess the ball are considered offensive.

Should the foul moves made are severe, the referees can flash either a yellow card or a red card to the offensive players. A yellow card means the players' actions have been marked and they had been warned while a red card means the players are out of the field. Two yellow cards equal a red card.

It is not that hard to understand the game and you can master it simply by watching a few matches.

# 10. Baseball: Easy Rules to Play the Game

There are so many varieties of sports available today to the extent that sometimes you get hesitant on the type of sports you should be joining instead of the ways to play a certain type of sport game. If you are currently having a headache on which sports game to join, why not try out baseball as a starter point first?

Baseball is not a tough sport to learn, and if you have enough passion and determination, you are guaranteed to be able to master the sports game of baseball in no time.

Let us start off with the overall description of this sport. What exactly is baseball? What is so interesting about it compared to the other sports and games? This little story will help you in understanding the ultimate excitement of baseball as an all-time favorite sports until today.

Before you are pumped up, here are some simple explanations on baseball. Basically, there are two teams in total in a baseball game, with each team having nine players. Baseball is usually played on a baseball field. On this baseball field, there will be four bases, and each of these bases will form a line, joining up the starting point and the ending point of the field. We call the starting point of the baseball field a home plate. In addition, in this home plate, there are four sides that you must be alert on. The four bases are positioned in a situation as such:

First base – right side of the field.

Second base – top of the infield.

Third base – left side of the field.

Fourth base - the home plate.

To make it simple, the ultimate goal of a baseball game is to score more runs than the opponent team. Each team player will get a chance to become the batter of the team and here, his/her goal is to score a run that will worth one point. When the batter swings the baseball, the opponent team will have one player defending the baseball so as to disallow the batter to successfully swing the baseball in scoring a goal. In the same time, a catcher (same team as the batter) will be standing by behind the opponent team's player who will be defending the ball. The catcher will catch any balls that the opponent team's player does not hit and in the same time, he/she will signal the batter on the desired direction to throw the ball.

The batter of the game will get three strikes until he/she is out from the game. After hitting the ball, the batter will then start running, and by this, he/she will no longer be called a batter, but he/she will then be referred to as the runner, who will thus attempt to reach a base, and once reaching a base, he/she will be safe in the base until the next batter comes up to take his/her place. Meanwhile, in order to prevent this from happening, the opponent team will put the runners out using the ball, which the runner will have to leave the field if he/she is hit by the ball.

# 11. Racquetball: Simple & Basic Rules

If you are having a hard time deciding on which sports to play during your free time, why not try out racquetball? Racquetball is the ideal sport for individuals who dislike spending too much time outside and prefer to have more privacy playing sports in an indoor environment. Racquetball is somehow slightly similar to squash and tennis; however, there are certain rules of racquetball that allows it to be different from squash and tennis, as well as making it more enjoyable.

Racquetball is not a difficult sport to play; in fact, racquetball is one of the easiest sports to play! The main idea of racquetball is to keep hitting the ball so that your opponent is not able to retrieve it before the ball bounces back twice. By this, your stamina and energy level become important factors in determining if you can win the game because racquetball will require you to run a lot throughout the whole game to stop your opponent from winning.

One of the most important rules of racquetball is that the ball must hit the front wall before you hit the ball back to the way to qualify it for points scoring. The ball must also be hit to return to the wall before it bounces twice in the floor. In certain cases, there are also situations when rally happens, which means the exchange between you and your opponent. One way to fail your opponent is to make sure that your opponent is unable to retrieve your shot before the second bounce. Another way to fail your opponent is to strategize your hit properly and make sure that the hit given by your opponent when the ball bounces back is unable to meet the front wall and hitting it into the floor instead.

The scoring system of racquetball is fairly simple. Only the person serving (the person hitting the ball) can contribute in earning more scores. There are also two types of situations, which will cause the game to stop. One of them is when you or your opponent runs into each other, or a situation when the ball hits either you or your opponent, which may lead to a certain extent of injury. Another situation that may cause the game to stop is when tricky situations appear, such as you or your opponent purposely hinders each other, or purposely blocking each other to carry out a shot.

Racquetball is not a difficult game to understand. The best way to master this game is through constant practice. Once you are familiar with the game, you are then ready to challenge any of your friends and eventually, the sport might just become your favorite sport at the end of the day! The most important thing to remember in racquetball is to make sure that you always have your stamina trained and that you must always remember the basic rules of the game which will cause you to lose your point or causing the game to stop halfway.

# 12. Dodge Ball: How to Play Dodge Ball

Dodge ball is a fun pastime that we all have seen children play. It is a very simple game and even adults can enjoy the occasional game of Dodge ball. So how do you play a game like this? Simply choose two teams with at least six members each. Finding a field to play on is the next idea.

Volleyball and basketball courts without nets are a great place to have a game. Have a court marked with lines on all four sides and a line down the middle. Selection of the ball is the next step of this game.

Lightweight balls of rubber are your best choice as if you get hit with a volleyball in the face you are going to be hurting your friend! The OUCH factor has to be taken into consideration. This is where choosiness and caution when selecting a ball to play with are warranted. Too light and the bounce factor is out of this world. Too heavy and you are going to have bruises! Now the next thing would be to line the two teams up on opposite sides of the court.

Choosing which team goes first in this game means a coin toss.

The object of the game is to hit the opposite team with the Dodge ball before they hit all your team members. Game rules vary greatly here. Players that are out meaning being hit with the ball are able to leave the playing area. In addition, if an opposing team member hits a team member of yours above the head, well, they are then out. Sometimes you can use time outs in this game. However, one sneaky way to get someone out without hitting them is to catch the thrown ball! Eliminating the opposing team is the name of the game here.

It is a fast-paced game that both kids and some adults enjoy. The players are constantly moving all the time during the game so if you are a little out of shape, this will definitely get you back into it! It is a great game to play and if you follow the rules, good clean fun can be had by all. However, remember that the game is good clean fun, not target practice! Getting carried away can cause a lot of problems with team members. There really is not a limit on Dodge ball teams. However, most will start out at six members apiece.

The only limiting factor is the field of play. Therefore, you really do not need any equipment except the Dodge ball. This means this game can be played most anywhere without special equipment needed.

# 13. How to Play Horse Shoes

Ah, horseshoes! A simply wonderful game that is associated with older folks playing it. It does not need much equipment, just two sticks or metal poles and four horseshoes. Divide folks into two teams and each team receives two horseshoes. Who goes first is next up.

Once you are in the horseshoe court, the first team player will toss both of the horseshoes from behind the line designating foul. Then both horseshoes are thrown by one member of the other team. Scoring is as follows: 1 point is awarded for a horseshoe at least six inches away.

This basically means that the item must be that length to the stake. Leaners are also awarded one point. Ringers, which are shoes that wrap around the stake, get 3 points. Sometimes leaners are awarded 2 points by those that do not play professionally. Then this will follow with the next one from each time. Their points will also be added to the scores of the first pair. Throwing should be done from each end of the court until all have tossed horseshoes. An inning is marked in this fashion for horseshoes. So what is the limit for points?

This will depend on if the game is a point limit or a shoe limit. Forty shoes will constitute a winning team with shoe limit while 40 points will constitute a winner in point limit. Extra innings may be needed in event of a tie. The team with the highest score wins the game of horseshoes. This simple game is among the best ever created for pleasure. With very little materials needed, it is a simple game that just about anyone can catch onto very quickly. All you would have to truly know would be the how-to of setting up your horseshoe court.

A regulation horseshoe pit has to be a length of 46 feet by a width of 6 feet. Two areas are marked at about 40 feet for the two stakes. Pits should be dug up to 72 inches long, up to 36 inches wide and up to 8 inches deep. Pits need to be filled and leveled so that the playing surface is level. Sawdust is a good leveler for the pits. Stakes are then placed into their prospective pits and extend 15 inches above the surface of the pit.

Foul lines would then need to be set. This is basically how you set up horseshoes and a horseshoe pit for playing the game of horseshoes. It is a very deceptively easy game to play that can be hours of fun!

# 14. How to Play Lacrosse

Lacrosse is the hottest game out there. Scoring more points in the game is the object here. Similarity to football in the fact that it has four quarters is well marked. The length of time for these quarters depends greatly upon the players involved. Each team has to switch ends once a quarter is over with. NCAA rules states that a lacrosse field is "110 yards by 60 yards". Nets for the goals are 6X6 and are positioned from the end line 15 yards.

Teams of Lacrosse are 10 people each. The positions are as follows: Goalie – 1, Defenders – 3, Attack men – 3 and Midfielders – 3. In game play, one player each from the team will face-off in a position of hands and feet with sticks, then use different methods to get possession. Once the ball is picked up, it is considered possession. Bear in mind that you cannot use hands in this game. Only the sticks can be used. Once the player with possession gets the ball into the opposing net, then a goal and one point are given. Those on offense run or pass the ball to team members. No offside action is allowed with this game.

The crease area can only be entered by defensive players. If an offensive member enters, then possession shifts to the opposing team. Timing is everything when it comes to playing this game. Goalies only have 4 seconds to get the ball out of the crease before losing possession. Offense has 20 seconds midfield crossing, and 10 seconds to move into the area of attack. This is a very physical game and body as well as stick checks is common. This is basically trying to engage an opponent's stick. Body checks are allowed above the waist and below the neck.

The game has several different penalties that you should know about such as personal and technical fouls. Illegal Cross Checking, tripping, slashing all give one minute penalties while Warding Off, thumbing, crease violations and off sides are all technical violations that cause the loss of possession to the team in question. Before you play the game of Lacrosse learning the rules and whatnot is smart. It is a fast-paced game that athletes enjoy and it makes for a great game to watch. Different equipment such as helmets, sticks, gloves and kneepads are often needed.

This game is not too difficult to learn. It can be a very fulfilling game to play and requires the most out of any athlete that plays this particular game both professionally and in amateur play.

# 15. How to Play Volleyball

Volleyball is a very easy game to play and takes little equipment to work with. There are five simple steps to play volleyball and they run as follows: Ball serve, ball return, keep the ball from hitting the floor on the team side, be careful of out-of-bounds and do not hit a ball that is going this way.

Equipment needed is a volleyball, net and kneepads. Six team members are all that is needed in order to play any version of volleyball. Learning how to serve is the most difficult part of the game.

Service can be underhand or overhand depending on experience. Bumping and setting are also useful skills to learn. Bumping requires the use of locked arms while setting requires using your fingertips to hit the ball. Spiking is another great skill to learn. It is a simple maneuver such as holding up a hand and smacking the ball down over the net. Spiking is not required of a beginner in volleyball and there is more than one-way to do a spike. A jumping spike requires a bit more force and can also be easily learned as your skills progress.

Passing, Digging and blocking are all skills that should be learned. Passing simply means to handle the serve that has been serviced properly and return it back to the opponent. Digging means to prevent the ball from touching the floor, while blocking happens at the net to stop or alter the movement of the ball. In team play, each team member rotates to be a server during the game. As far as scoring goes, the first team to reach 25 would be the winner. However, the rules are different between leagues, levels and tournaments.

Three different formations are always there in volleyball. For example, take 4-2. Two setters and four hitters are present in this formation. 6-2 is where one team member moves forward from their previous position. This setup also requires two setters similar to the 4-2 configuration. The final set up is the 5-1 configuration, which means that this rotation has only setter regardless of where he or she may be. This too is a very active game that demands plenty of energy on the player's part. Other types of volleyball include beach volleyball and beach ball volleyball is still in existence today. Bear in mind that there are five different positions in volleyball today.

These positions include Defensive/Libero specialist, right side or opposite hitter, middle hitter, Left side hitter/outside hitter and setter. The specific functions of play during games fall to those team players.

# 16. Boxing

A lot of people often associate boxing as a violent sport. The idea of having two men fighting and punching each other in a stage sounds very brutal and it is indeed brutal. However, there is something redemptive about boxing that most of us often overlook and it is that this is a sport that requires dedication and determination.

Boxing is a sport filled with underdogs rising to the needs of the people, where many people find hope and will to survive through boxing. A lot of great boxers of the world often came from the slum and they often represented hope to the regular folks that if they can succeed in lives, are it through boxing or other means, there is still hope regardless how desperate the situation may be.

Generally, boxing is a game of a combative fight between two fighters or boxers using nothing but their fists in a stage. While it is basically a game of fighting, there are rules and regulations that govern the game so that it is fair to both the fighters and to ensure both of them play fair. A referee often joins the two fighters on stage, making sure that there are no dirty tricks pulled by either of the fighters and that the game is fair. Other than that, the function of the referee is also to ensure that should either one of the boxers raise the white flag or that he or she was knocked out, the standing one would not continue with his or her assaults.

There are rounds in boxing and each round usually consists of three minutes of boxing and each game consists of about twelve rounds. Both boxers would give their bests within these three minutes and once the bell rang, signifying the end of the round, both of them have to go back to their respective corners and rest or reflect back on their games.

When the bell strikes again, both the players can resume with the fights. There are two types of boxing, namely, the amateur and the professional. For the amateur boxing, there is a point system where points will be awarded for each clean blow. Other than that, headgears are a must for amateur boxing. As for the professional boxing, headgears are not allowed and that should the referee deem the fighters unfit to defend themselves, he can stop the match. Normally, professional fighters are bare-chested.

There are many rules and you need to take a lot of time to fully understand it. One of the major rules is that it is not allowed to hit below the belts of the fighters and there is no spitting, pushing, biting, holding and tripping. Boxing is a very dangerous sport and safety precautions should be employed first before entering the stage.

Vince Stead has been raising dogs for over 25 years now, and served in the United States Navy for 8 years from 1982 to 1990. He has worked for himself for the last 20 years, and lives in Southern California.

# Other Books by Vince Stead

Sammy the Runaway Mastiff
ISBN# 1-59824-314-4


The Back Yard Kids Club
ISBN# 978-1456406219


How to Get Even and Revenge with Pranks on Anyone
ISBN# 978-1-45387-727-2


Navy Fun
ISBN# 978-1-59824-514-1


Navy Sea Stories
ISBN# 978-1456558666


**In addition, many different dog breed training books under Vince Stead's name.**

Printed in Great Britain
by Amazon.co.uk, Ltd.,
Marston Gate.